BAVARIAN COOKING

A BAVARIAN COOKBOOK WITH AUTHENTIC BAVARIAN RECIPES

By
BookSumo Press
Copyright © by Saxonberg Associates

Published by
BookSumo Press, a DBA of Saxonberg Associates
http://www.booksumo.com/

About the Author.

BookSumo Press is a publisher of unique, easy, and healthy cookbooks.

Our cookbooks span all topics and all subjects. If you want a deep dive into the possibilities of cooking with any type of ingredient. Then BookSumo Press is your go to place for robust yet simple and delicious cookbooks and recipes. Whether you are looking for great tasting pressure cooker recipes or authentic ethic and cultural food. BookSumo Press has a delicious and easy cookbook for you.

With simple ingredients, and even simpler step-by-step instructions BookSumo cookbooks get everyone in the kitchen chefing delicious meals.

BookSumo is an independent publisher of books operating in the beautiful Garden State (NJ) and our team of chefs and kitchen experts are here to teach, eat, and be merry!

INTRODUCTION

Welcome to *The Effortless Chef Series*! Thank you for taking the time to purchase this cookbook.

Come take a journey into the delights of easy cooking. The point of this cookbook and all BookSumo Press cookbooks is to exemplify the effortless nature of cooking simply.

In this book we focus on Bavarian cooking. You will find that even though the recipes are simple, the taste of the dishes are quite amazing.

So will you take an adventure in simple cooking? If the answer is yes please consult the table of contents to find the dishes you are most interested in.

Once you are ready, jump right in and start cooking.

— BookSumo Press

TABLE OF CONTENTS

Any Issues? Contact Us

If you find that something important to you is missing from this book please contact us at info@booksumo.com.

We will take your concerns into consideration when the 2nd edition of this book is published. And we will keep you updated!

— BookSumo Press

LEGAL NOTES

COMMON ABBREVIATIONS

cup(s)	C.
tablespoon	tbsp
teaspoon	tsp
ounce	oz.
pound	lb

*All units used are standard American measurements

Chapter 1: Easy Bavarian Recipes

Bavarian Pretzel Bread

Ingredients

DOUGH

- 1 1/3 C. warm water (105-115 degrees)
- 2 tbsp warm milk
- 2 1/2 tsp active dry yeast
- 1/3 C. light brown sugar
- 2 tbsp butter, melted
- 4 C. all-purpose flour
- kosher salt

PARBOILING LIQUID

- 2 quarts cold water
- baking soda (1/2 C.)

Directions

- In the bowl of a standing electric mixer fitted with a dough hook, add 1/3 C. of the warm water and yeast and mix till foamy.

- Add the milk, remaining cup of warm water, melted butter and sugar and swirl till sugar is dissolved.
- Add flour and mix on medium-low speed till a firm, pliable dough ball is formed.
- Place dough onto a lightly floured surface and with your hands, knead for about 2 minutes.
- Now, roll the dough into a 2 foot long log and then, cut into 12 equal sized pieces.
- With a plastic wrap, cover the dough and then, cover with a damp cloth. Keep aside for about 10 minutes.
- With your hands, pat the dough into rolls. Place rolls onto a lightly floured surface in a single layer about 1-inch apart.
- With a lightly greased plastic wrap, cover the dough rolls. Keep aside for about 30 minutes. arrange racks in upper and middle portions of oven.
- Set your oven to 425 degrees F and lightly, grease 2 baking sheets.
- In a large pan, add cold water and bring to a rolling boil and stir in baking soda.
- Place the rolls in batches, 2 at a time in the boiling water and boil for about 30 seconds, flipping once.
- With a slotted spoon, carefully remove the rolls from pan to drain.
- Sprinkle each ball with the salt lightly.
- Arrange the rolls onto greased baking sheets in a single layer and cook in the oven for about 8-10 minutes,

shifting pans from top to bottom and back to front once in the middle way.

- Remove from the oven and keep onto the wire rack to cool in the pan for about 5 minutes.
- Serve warm or at room temperature.

Servings Per Recipe: 12

Timing Information:

Preparation	35 mins
Total Time	1 hr 54 mins

Nutritional Information:

Calories	196.1
Fat	2.4g
Cholesterol	5.4mg
Sodium	26.6mg
Carbohydrates	38.2g
Protein	4.7g

* Percent Daily Values are based on a 2,000 calorie diet.

Bavarian Fruit and Vanilla Cream Cheese Torte

Ingredients

BASE

- 1/2 C. butter
- 1/3 C. sugar
- 1/4 tsp vanilla
- 1 C. flour
- 1/4 C. raspberry jam

FILLING

- 8 oz. cream cheese
- 1/4 C. sugar
- 1 egg
- 1/2 tsp vanilla

TOPPING

- 1/3 C. sugar
- 1/2 tsp cinnamon
- 4 C. apples, peeled,cored & sliced
- 1/2 C. sliced almonds

Directions

- Set your oven to 450 degrees F before doing anything else.
- For the base: in a bowl, add the sugar, butter and vanilla extract and beat till foamy.
- Add the flour and mix till well combined.
- Place the mixture into a 9-inch spring form pan and press to smooth.
- Spread the jam over the flour mixture evenly.
- For the filling: in a bowl, add the sugar and cream cheese and beat till smooth.
- Add egg and vanilla extract and mix well.
- Place filling mixture over jam evenly.
- For the topping: in a bowl, add apples, sugar and cinnamon and toss to coat well.
- Spread the apple mixture over the filling mixture evenly and sprinkle with the almonds.
- Cook in the oven for about 10 minutes.
- Now, set your oven to 400 degrees F and cook for about 25 minutes.
- Remove from oven and keep aside to cool before serving.

Servings Per Recipe: 6

Timing Information:

Preparation	20 mins
Total Time	55 mins

Nutritional Information:

Calories	597.5
Fat	33.2g
Cholesterol	113.3mg
Sodium	274.4mg
Carbohydrates	70.6g
Protein	7.5g

* Percent Daily Values are based on a 2,000 calorie diet.

Obatzda

(Bavarian Brie Cheese Spread)

Ingredients

- 1 lb. Brie cheese, coarsely chopped
- 6 oz. cream cheese
- 1/4 C. butter, cut into small pieces
- 1/4 C. dark German ale
- 3 cloves roasted garlic
- 1 tsp caraway seed
- 1 pinch sweet paprika
- salt & freshly ground black pepper
- 1/4 C. diced Spanish onion
- 1 loaf French bread
- 1/3 C. thinly sliced red onions (for garnishing)
- 1/4 C. thinly sliced radish (for garnishing)
- cut vegetables, such as carrots or celery sticks, sliced bell peppers and bit sized florets of broccoli and cauliflower
- 1/2 lb. mixed olives

Directions

- Set your oven to 375 degrees F before doing anything else.

- Carefully, remove any papery coating from the garlic head.
- With a large sharp knife, cut about 1/2-inch portion from the top of the garlic bulb, exposing the tips of the garlic cloves.
- In a small baking dish, arrange garlic garlic bulb and lightly, drizzle with olive oil.
- Sprinkle with the salt and add 1/4 C. of the water in the bottom of baking dish.
- With a piece of foil, cover the baking dish tightly and cook in the oven for about 1 hour.
- In a bowl, add the Brie cheese, cream cheese, ale, butter, garlic, caraway seeds, paprika, salt and pepper and beat till well combined.
- In a strainer, add the diced onion and rinse under cold water.
- Drain the onion completely and with a clean kitchen towel, squeeze out all the moisture.
- Add the onion into the cheese mixture and gently, stir to combine.
- Refrigerate, covered for at least 2 hours.
- Slice French bread into 1/4-inch thick slices.
- Place Vidalia onion over dip, followed by radish slices, fresh cut vegetables, olives and bread slices.

Servings Per Recipe: 8

Timing Information:

| Preparation | 15 mins |
| Total Time | 2 hrs 15 mins |

Nutritional Information:

Calories	727.0
Fat	34.2g
Cholesterol	95.4mg
Sodium	1343.9mg
Carbohydrates	77.1g
Protein	28.7g

* Percent Daily Values are based on a 2,000 calorie diet.

Bavarian Borretsch

(Red Radish and Onion Salad)

Ingredients

- 1 head lettuce
- 1 C. watercress (rocket)
- 1 small red onion, diced
- 8 -10 small red radishes
- 3 tbsp fresh borage leaves, chopped plus more for garnishing
- freshly grated black pepper

DRESSING

- 2 tbsp white wine vinegar
- 1 pinch salt
- 2 tbsp walnut oil

Directions

- For the dressing in a non-reactive container, add all ingredients and mix well. Keep aside for at least 1 hour before using.
- Wash the lettuce and watercress completely and spin dry.
- In a large salad bowl, mix together the salad ingredients.

- Add the dressing and toss to coat.
- Serve with a garnishing of the additional borage leaves and flowers.

Servings Per Recipe: 4

Timing Information:

Preparation	10 mins
Total Time	10 mins

Nutritional Information:

Calories	82.5
Fat	6.9g
Cholesterol	0.0mg
Sodium	69.5mg
Carbohydrates	4.5g
Protein	1.6g

* Percent Daily Values are based on a 2,000 calorie diet.

Laugenbrezeln

(Homemade Bavarian Pretzels)

Ingredients

- 3 3/4-4 C. unbleached bread flour
- 3 tbsp unsalted butter, chilled, cut into 1/4 inch pieces
- 1 1/4 C. warm water (70-78 degrees)
- 1 tsp instant yeast
- 2 1/4 tsp sea salt
- 1/3 C. baking soda (for boiling the rolls)
- kosher salt (for topping) (optional)
- sesame seeds (for topping) (optional)

Directions

- In the bowl of a stand mixer with a paddle attachment, place the flour and butter on low speed till a coarse cornmeal like mixture is formed.
- Add water and sprinkle with the yeast and salt.
- Now, attach to the dough hook and knead on medium speed till very smooth and pliable.
- Make a ball from the dough and transfer in a large well greased bowl.

- With a plastic wrap, cover the bowl and keep aside in a warm place for about 1 hour.
- Lightly, grease a baking sheet.
- Place the dough onto an unfloured surface and with your hands, pat into a rough rectangle.
- Cut the dough rectangle into 8 equal sized portions.
- Now, shape the dough portions into pretzels.
- Arrange the pretzels onto the prepared baking sheet in a single layer about 1-inch apart.
- With a plastic wrap, cover the baking sheet and refrigerator for about 2-24 hours.
- Set your oven to 350 degrees F and grease a baking dish.
- In a wide 6 quart kettle, add 4 quarts of the water and bring to a boil.
- Slowly, stir in the baking soda and reduce the heat to a healthy simmer.
- Add the pretzels in batches, 3-4 at a time and cook for about 20 seconds per side.
- With a slotted spoon, remove the rolls to drain.
- Arrange the rolls onto the prepared baking sheet and sprinkle with the salt and sesame seeds.
- Cook in the oven for about 30-35 minutes.
- Remove from the oven and keep onto the wire rack to cool in the pan for about 10 minutes.

Servings Per Recipe: 8

Timing Information:

Preparation	3 hrs
Total Time	3 hrs 30 mins

Nutritional Information:

Calories	274.8
Fat	5.5g
Cholesterol	11.4mg
Sodium	3209.1mg
Carbohydrates	47.2g
Protein	8.3g

* Percent Daily Values are based on a 2,000 calorie diet.

CUCUMBER AND MUSTARD SALAD FROM BAVARIA

Ingredients

- 2 medium cucumbers, thinly sliced
- 4 green onions, thinly sliced
- 3 small tomatoes, sliced
- 2 tbsp fresh parsley, chopped

FOR THE DRESSING

- 1/4 C. sour cream
- 1/4 tsp prepared mustard
- 2 tbsp minced fresh dill
- 1 tbsp vinegar
- 1 tbsp milk
- 1/2 tsp salt
- 1/8 tsp pepper

Directions

- In a large salad bowl, mix together tomatoes, onions, cucumbers and parsley.
- For the dressing: in another bowl, add all ingredients and beat till well combined.

- Place dressing over salad and gently, toss to coat.
- Refrigerate, covered to chill for at least 1 hour before serving.

Servings Per Recipe: 6

Timing Information:

Preparation	10 mins
Total Time	1 hr 10 mins

Nutritional Information:

Calories	49.8
Fat	2.3g
Cholesterol	4.5mg
Sodium	209.2mg
Carbohydrates	6.8g
Protein	1.6g

* Percent Daily Values are based on a 2,000 calorie diet.

Bavarian Garlic and Cheese Spread

Ingredients

- 1 oz. shallot, minced finely
- 1 garlic clove, minced finely
- 3 1/2 oz. cottage cheese
- 3 1/2 oz. cream cheese
- 3 1/2 oz. butter, softened
- 3 1/2 oz. Brie cheese, chopped roughly
- 1 tsp paprika
- 1/2 tsp seasoning salt
- 2 dashes pepper

Directions

- In a food processor, add all ingredients and pulse on medium speed till smooth and creamy with some small lumps.
- Transfer into a bowl and refrigerate to chill before serving.
- Serve alongside the crackers.

Servings Per Recipe: 10

Timing Information:

| Preparation | 15 mins |
| Total Time | 2 hrs 15 mins |

Nutritional Information:

Calories	148.6
Fat	14.3g
Cholesterol	41.2mg
Sodium	225.8mg
Carbohydrates	1.5g
Protein	3.9g

* Percent Daily Values are based on a 2,000 calorie diet.

Zwetschgenkuchen

(Plum Cake Bavarian)

Ingredients

FOR THE DOUGH

- 4 C. all-purpose flour
- 1/2 C. unsalted butter
- 1 egg
- 1/4 C. sugar, plus
- 1 tbsp sugar
- 1/4 oz. active dry yeast
- 1/4 tsp salt
- 1 C. milk, lukewarm

FOR THE CRUMB TOPPING (OPTIONAL)

- 1 C. unsalted butter, cut into tiny cubes
- 1 C. sugar
- 2 -3 tbsp vanilla sugar
- 1 1/2-2 1/2 C. flour

ADDITIONAL Ingredients

- 2 lb. plums (Italian Prune Plums)
- 2 -3 tsp sugar

- whipped cream, for garnish (optional)

Directions

- For the dough: in a small bowl, add half of the milk, yeast, 2 tbsp of the flour and 1 tsp of the sugar and mix well. Keep aside for at least 1 hour.
- In a large bowl, add the remaining dough ingredients and mix well.
- Add the yeast mixture and mix till a smooth dough is formed.
- Now with your hands, knead the dough and keep aside in a warm place till doubles in volume.
- Roll the dough in the size that will fit into the baking sheet.
- Place the dough onto a greased baking sheet.
- Wash the plums and remove any stems. Then, cut each plum in half and remove pits.
- Arrange plum halves over the dough evenly, stem-side up and sprinkle with the sugar.
- For the topping: in a bowl, add the butter and sugars and mix.
- Slowly, add the flour and mix till a dry and crumbly mixture is formed.
- Sprinkle crumb mixture over the plums evenly and keep aside for about 30 minutes.
- Set your oven to 350 degrees F.

- Cook in the oven for about 30-40 minutes.
- Remove from the oven and keep onto the wire rack to cool in the pan for about 5-10 minutes.
- Carefully, invert the cake onto the wire rack to cool completely.
- Serve with a topping of the dollop of the whipped cream

Servings Per Recipe: 12

Timing Information:

Preparation	1 hr
Total Time	4 hrs

Nutritional Information:

Calories	561.3
Fat	24.9g
Cholesterol	79.3mg
Sodium	69.3mg
Carbohydrates	76.4g
Protein	8.1g

* Percent Daily Values are based on a 2,000 calorie diet.

Potato Salad Bavarian

Ingredients

- 4 C. potatoes, peeled and sliced 1/4 inch thick
- 2 C. chicken broth
- 1 C. bacon, chopped
- 1/2 C. onion, minced
- 1 tsp sugar
- 2 tbsp lemon juice
- 1 tbsp Dijon mustard
- 1/2 C. flat leaf parsley, chopped

Directions

- In a small pan, add the stock and potatoes and bring to a gentle boil.
- Cook till the potatoes become tender but still retain their shape.
- Drain the potatoes, reserving some stock in a bowl.
- Meanwhile, heat a skillet and cook the bacon till crisp.
- Transfer the crisp onto a plate, reserving the bacon fat.
- In a large bowl, add the lemon juice, sugar, Dijon mustard and 4 tbsp of the warm bacon fa and beat till smooth.

- Add the bacon, potatoes, onions, parsley, salt and pepper and toss to coat. (You can add a little of the reserved chicken broth to moisten the mixture).
- Keep aside in the room temperature for about 2 hours before serving.

Servings Per Recipe: 4

Timing Information:

Preparation	15 mins
Total Time	30 mins

Nutritional Information:

Calories	318.8
Fat	17.2g
Cholesterol	24.4mg
Sodium	729.8mg
Carbohydrates	31.0g
Protein	10.3g

* Percent Daily Values are based on a 2,000 calorie diet.

FULL BAVARIAN DINNER

(COUNTRY VEGETABLES AND BEEF ROAST)

Ingredients

- 3 lb. boneless beef chuck roast, trimmed
- 1 tbsp cooking oil
- 2 C. sliced carrots
- 2 C. chopped onions
- 1 C. sliced celery
- 3/4 C. chopped kosher-style dill pickle
- 1/2 C. dry red wine
- 1/3 C. German mustard
- 1/2 tsp coarse ground black pepper
- 1/4 tsp ground cloves
- 2 bay leaves
- 2 tbsp all-purpose flour
- 4 tbsp dry red wine
- cooked pasta, of your choice
- crumbled cooked bacon (optional)

Directions

- In a large skillet, heat 1 tbsp of the oil and sear the roast till browned.
- Drain off the grease.
- In a small bowl, mix together the 1/2 C. of the red wine, mustard, pepper, cloves and bay leaves.
- In the bottom of a slow cooker, place the carrots, celery, onions and 3/4 C. of the pickles and top with the browned roast.
- Place wine mixture over meat mixture.
- Set the slow cooker on Low and cook, covered for about 8-10 hours.
- With a slotted spoon, transfer the meat and vegetables onto a serving platter and with a piece of foil, cover to keep warm.
- Discard the bay leaves.
- For gravy: transfer the liquid from slow cooker into a small pan and skim off extra fat.
- In a small shaker, add 4 tbsp of the red wine and 2 tbsp of the flour and shake till well combined.
- Place the pan of liquid on medium-high heat and stir in the flour mixture.
- Cook till gravy becomes thick, stirring continuously.
- Divide meat, vegetables and pasta onto serving plates.
- Serve with a topping of the gravy.

Servings Per Recipe: 8

Timing Information:

| Preparation | 20 mins |
| Total Time | 10 hrs 20 mins |

Nutritional Information:

Calories	507.2
Fat	35.1g
Cholesterol	117.3mg
Sodium	303.6mg
Carbohydrates	9.7g
Protein	32.3g

* Percent Daily Values are based on a 2,000 calorie diet.

OLD GERMAN FLANK

Ingredients

- 1 1/2 lb. flank steaks
- 1 potato, shredded
- 1 tbsp onion, chopped
- 1 tbsp green bell pepper, seeded and chopped
- 1 tsp pimiento, chopped
- 1 tsp parsley, chopped
- kitchen string
- 3 tbsp canola oil
- 1 can onion soup
- 1 1/2 tbsp cornstarch
- 1/2 C. water

Directions

- With a sharp knife, cut 1/4-inch deep slits in flank steak in a crosshatch pattern across both sides.
- In a bowl, mix together potato, onion, bell pepper, pimiento, parsley and salt.
- Place potato mixture over meat and roll up. With a kitchen string, tie the roll to secure the filling.
- In a heavy non-stick skillet, heat the oil on medium-high heat and sear the steak roll for about 2 minutes per side.

- Discard the drippings from pan.
- Add the onion soup and stir to combine.
- Reduce the heat to very low and simmer, covered for about 1 1/2 hours.
- Transfer roll onto a serving platter.
- Transfer the pan juices into a glass bowl and add enough water to equal 1 C.
- In another small bowl, dissolve cornstarch into 1/2 cup of the water.
- In a pan, add the cornstarch mixture and pan juices over medium heat and cook till thick, stirring continuously.
- Cut the meat roll into 1-inch slices crosswise.
- Serve with a topping of the sauce.

Servings Per Recipe: 4

Timing Information:

Preparation	15 mins
Total Time	1 hr 45 mins

Nutritional Information:

Calories	462.0
Fat	25.7g
Cholesterol	69.7mg
Sodium	737.0mg
Carbohydrates	17.4g
Protein	39.5g

* Percent Daily Values are based on a 2,000 calorie diet.

GROUND BEEF MEATBALLS WITH MUSHROOMS

Ingredients

- 6 tbsp chopped onions
- 3 tsp butter
- 3 slices bread, torn into small pieces
- 3 tbsp milk
- 1 1/2 tsp prepared yellow mustard
- 1 tsp salt
- 3 -5 dashes black pepper
- 1 1/2 lb. lean ground beef
- 1 (8 oz.) cans mushroom stems and pieces, undrained
- 6 store bought gingersnap cookies, crushed with a rolling pin
- 1/2 C. water
- 3 tbsp packed brown sugar
- 1 1/2 tsp beef bouillon granules

Directions

- Set your oven to 350 degrees F before doing anything else and lightly, grease a 2-1/2 quart rectangular baking dish.
- In a skillet, melt the butter and sauté the onion till tender.

- Transfer onion into a bowl with beef, torn bread, milk, mustard, salt and pepper and mix well.
- Make about 29 (1-1/4-inch) sized meatballs.
- Arrange meatballs into the prepared baking dish in a single layer.
- In a small pan, add the mushrooms, gingersnaps, brown sugar, bouillon granules and water over medium heat and bring to a boil, stirring continuously.
- Cook till sauce becomes slightly thick, stirring continuously.
- Spread sauce over meatballs evenly.
- Cover the baking dish and cook in the oven for about 35 minutes.

Servings Per Recipe: 5

Timing Information:

Preparation	0 mins
Total Time	45 mins

Nutritional Information:

Calories	389.2
Fat	17.7g
Cholesterol	95.7mg
Sodium	949.6mg
Carbohydrates	26.2g
Protein	30.1g

* Percent Daily Values are based on a 2,000 calorie diet.

Bavarian Sauerkraut Sausage Stir Fry

Ingredients

- 1 lb. kielbasa, sliced
- 1 tbsp chopped onion
- 1 clove garlic, minced
- 1 C. sauerkraut, rinsed
- 2 C. water
- 1 C. rice, uncooked
- 2 tsp prepared mustard
- 2 tsp Worcestershire sauce
- 1 tsp salt
- 2 tsp caraway seeds
- 1/8 tsp pepper
- 1/8 tsp nutmeg

Directions

- Heat a large skillet and cook the kielbasa till browned.
- Stir in the onion and garlic and sauté till tender.
- Stir in the remaining ingredients and bring to a boil.
- Reduce the heat and simmer, covered for about 30 minutes.

Servings Per Recipe: 4

Timing Information:

Preparation	10 mins
Total Time	40 mins

Nutritional Information:

Calories	542.2
Fat	31.5g
Cholesterol	74.7mg
Sodium	1900.4mg
Carbohydrates	45.1g
Protein	17.8g

* Percent Daily Values are based on a 2,000 calorie diet.

OLD GERMAN RUMP ROAST

Ingredients

- 1 boneless beef rump (3 lb.)
- 3 tbsp stone ground mustard
- 1 tbsp creamy horseradish sauce
- 1 (7/8 oz.) package brown gravy mix
- 1/2 C. beer
- 1/2 C. water
- 3 tbsp all-purpose flour
- 1 tbsp chopped fresh chives

Directions

- Grease a 3 1/2-4 quart slow cooker with the cooking spray.
- In small bowl, add the mustard, horseradish sauce and gravy mix and mix well.
- In the slow cooker, place the beef roast and top with the mustard mixture evenly.
- Carefully, place the beer around the roast.
- Set the slow cooker on Low and cook, covered for about 9-10 hours.

- with a slotted spoon, transfer the roast onto a serving platter and with a piece of the foil, cover the late to keep warm.
- In a 2 quart pan, dissolve flour in the water over medium-high heat.
- Add the cooking juices from slow cooker and bring to a boil, stirring continuously.
- Stir in the chives.
- Cut the beef into desired sized slices and serve alongside the gravy.

Servings Per Recipe: 8

Timing Information:

Preparation	15 mins
Total Time	9 hrs 15 mins

Nutritional Information:

Calories	32.7
Fat	0.5g
Cholesterol	0.0mg
Sodium	220.1mg
Carbohydrates	5.0g
Protein	0.9g

* Percent Daily Values are based on a 2,000 calorie diet.

20 Min Bavarian Egg Noodle and Apple Dinner

Ingredients

- 4 C. uncooked medium egg noodles
- 1 tbsp olive oil
- 1 C. sliced onion
- 1 tsp caraway seed
- 2 C. granny smith apples, peeled, sliced
- 1 1/2 C. refrigerated sauerkraut, drained
- 1 (12 oz.) packages chicken, apple sausage cut into 1/2 - inch thick slices
- 1/2 C. reduced-fat-free chicken broth
- 1/4 C. sherry wine

Directions

- In a large pan of the boiling water, prepare the egg noodles according to the package's directions.
- Drain well and keep aside.
- Meanwhile in a large nonstick skillet, heat the olive oil on medium-high heat and cook the sliced onion and caraway seeds for about 4 minutes, stirring occasionally.

- Stir in the apple, sauerkraut and sausage and cook for about 5 minutes.
- Stir in the chicken broth and sherry and bring to a boil.
- Reduce heat to medium and cook for about 5 minutes.
- Divide the noodles in serving plate and serve with a topping of the sausage mixture.

Servings Per Recipe: 4

Timing Information:

Preparation	0 mins
Total Time	20 mins

Nutritional Information:

Calories	485.2
Fat	14.7g
Cholesterol	85.2mg
Sodium	401.8mg
Carbohydrates	57.4g
Protein	18.0g

* Percent Daily Values are based on a 2,000 calorie diet.

Bavarian Creamy Chicken Cutlets

Ingredients

- 6 boneless skinless chicken breast halves
- 5 tbsp flour
- 1/2 tsp salt
- 1/4 tsp pepper
- 1/3 C. oil
- 1 can cream of chicken soup
- 1 tbsp soy sauce
- 1/4 C. slivered almonds
- 1/2 C. beer
- 1 C. mushroom, sliced

Directions

- Set your oven to 350 degrees F before doing anything else.
- In a shallow dish, mix together the flour, salt and pepper.
- Coat the chicken breast halves with the flour mixture evenly.
- In a skillet, heat the oil and sear the chicken till browned from both sides.
- Meanwhile in a bowl, add the beer, soup, soy sauce, mushrooms and 2 tbsp of the almonds and mix well.

- Arrange chicken breast halves in a baking dish in a single layer and top with the mushroom mixture evenly.
- Cook in the oven for about 45 minutes, basting with the pan juices occasionally.
- Remove from the oven and sprinkle with the remaining almonds.
- Cook in the oven for about 15 minutes.

Servings Per Recipe: 6

Timing Information:

Preparation	20 mins
Total Time	1 hr 20 mins

Nutritional Information:

Calories	344.8
Fat	18.8g
Cholesterol	72.5mg
Sodium	772.6mg
Carbohydrates	10.8g
Protein	30.8g

* Percent Daily Values are based on a 2,000 calorie diet.

Sauerbraten

(Pepper and Clove Beef Roast)

Ingredients

- 1/2 C. red wine vinegar
- 1 3/4 C. red wine
- 2 C. sliced yellow onions
- 6 parsley stems
- 6 black peppercorns
- 3 bay leaves
- 6 whole cloves
- 1 1/2-2 lb. beef top round roast
- 1/2 C. flour
- 2 tsp salt
- 1 tsp fresh ground black pepper
- 2 tbsp vegetable oil
- 3/4 C. chopped seeded tomatoes
- 3/4 C. water (approximately)
- 2 tbsp cream sherry
- 1 tbsp light brown sugar, plus additional to taste
- 1 tbsp fresh lemon juice
- parsley sprig (to garnish)
- sour cream (to serve)

Directions

- In a double layer of the cheesecloth, wrap the parsley stems, peppercorns, bay leaves and cloves tightly.
- In a medium pan, add the onions, vinegar, 1 1/2 C. of the red wine and cheesecloth packet and bring to a boil.
- Remove from the heat and keep aside in the room temperature to cool.
- With a fork, prick the top round from all sides.
- In a large resealable plastic bag, add the beef and wine mixture.
- Seal the bag and shake to coat well.
- Refrigerate for about 3-4 days in the refrigerator, turning once or twice.
- Remove the bag from the refrigerator and keep in the room temperature for about 2 hours before cooking.
- Remove beef from the bag and with paper towels, pat dry.
- Through a strainer, strain the marinade in a bowl, reserving the onions.
- Discard the cheesecloth bag.
- Set your oven to 325 degrees F.
- In a large shallow dish, mix together the flour, salt and black pepper.
- Coat the beef with the flour mixture evenly.

- In a heavy, oven proof pan, heat the vegetable oil on medium-high heat and sear the beef for about 5 minutes per side. Remove extra fat from the pan.
- In the pan, add 1 C. of the strained marinade liquid, remaining 1/4 C. of the red wine, tomatoes, reserved onions and enough water that comes about 1/3 of the way up the side of the beef and bring to a boil and boil.
- Boil for about 5 minutes.
- With a lid, cover the pan and transfer into the oven.
- Cook in the oven for about 3 hours, flipping and spooning braising liquid over meat after every 30 minutes.
- With a slotted spoon, transfer beef into a plate and cover with a piece of foil to keep warm.
- Through a strainer, strain the braising liquid in a small pan and discard the solids. Remove grease from the liquid.
- In the pan, add the remaining marinade, sherry and the 1 tbsp of the brown sugar and bring to a boil.
- Cook for about 10 minutes.
- Stir in the additional brown sugar, lemon juice and required amount of the seasoning and remove from the heat.
- Cut the roast into 3/8-inch thick slices against the grain.
- In a serving platter, arrange the beef slices and top with the sauce.
- Garnish with the parsley sprigs and serve with the topping of the sour cream.

Servings Per Recipe: 4

Timing Information:

Preparation	72 hrs
Total Time	75 hrs

Nutritional Information:

Calories	568.4
Fat	21.2g
Cholesterol	117.3mg
Sodium	1287.3mg
Carbohydrates	30.5g
Protein	40.7g

* Percent Daily Values are based on a 2,000 calorie diet.

Bavarian Cabbage

Ingredients

- 1 tbsp vegetable oil
- 2 lb.s stewing beef
- 2 C. chopped onions
- 2 tsp caraway seeds
- 1/4 tsp pepper
- 1 bay leaf
- 2 C. beef stock
- 1/3 C. red wine vinegar
- 3 tbsp packed brown sugar
- 1 tbsp grated lemon rind
- 1/4 C. molasses
- 2 tbsp all-purpose flour
- 1 tsp ground ginger
- 1 tsp ground cinnamon
- 1/4 tsp ground cloves

RED CABBAGE

- 1 small red cabbage, shredded
- 1/2 C. red wine vinegar
- 2 apples, peeled and sliced
- 1/4 C. packed brown sugar
- 1 tbsp butter

- 1/4 tsp salt
- 2 onions
- 4 whole cloves

Directions

In a Dutch oven, heat the oil on medium-high heat and sear the beef in batches till browned.

Transfer the beef into a plate.

In the same pan, add the onions, caraway seeds, pepper and bay leaf and sauté for about 1 minute.

Add the beef stock and bring to a boil, stirring to scrape up the brown bits.

Add the beef and astir to combine.

Reduce the heat and simmer, covered for about 2 hours.

Stir in the vinegar, sugar and rind and simmer, uncovered for about 30 minutes, stirring occasionally.

In a small bowl, add the molasses, flour, ginger, cinnamon and cloves and mix till a paste is formed.

Add about 2 tbsp of the stew juices and stir to combine.

Slowly, add the flour mixture into stew, beating continuously.

Cook on medium-high heat for about 3-5 minutes, stirring continuously.

Discard the bay leaf.

Meanwhile for the cabbage: in a large pan, add the cabbage, 1/2 C. of the water, vinegar, apples, brown sugar, butter and salt and mix till well combined.

Chop 1 of the onions and stir in the cabbage mixture.

Stick cloves into the remaining onion and insert in the cabbage mixture.

Cover the pan and bring to boil.

Reduce the heat and simmer for about 1 1/2 hours, stirring occasionally.

Discard clove studded onion.

Serve the cabbage alongside the stew.

Servings Per Recipe: 6

Timing Information:

Preparation	20 mins
Total Time	3 hrs 50 mins

Nutritional Information:

Calories	628.9
Fat	33.9g
Cholesterol	106.3mg
Sodium	496.8mg
Carbohydrates	51.6g
Protein	31.2g

* Percent Daily Values are based on a 2,000 calorie diet.

Easy Bavarian Meatballs Soup

Ingredients

- 1 egg, lightly beaten
- 1/2 C. soft breadcrumbs
- 3 tbsp dried parsley flakes
- 1/4 tsp ground allspice
- 1/4 tsp ground nutmeg
- 1/4 tsp pepper
- 1 1/2 lb. ground beef, crumbles
- 2 (14 1/2 oz.) cans beef broth
- 1 (14 1/2 oz.) cans diced tomatoes, undrained
- 1 (14 oz.) cans Bavarian sauerkraut, rinsed and well drained
- 2 medium potatoes, peeled and cubed
- 2 medium carrots, sliced
- 2 celery ribs, sliced
- 1 (1 oz.) envelope onion soup mix
- 1 tbsp sugar
- 1/2 tsp pepper
- 1 bay leaf

Directions

- Set your oven to 400 degrees F before doing anything else and arrange a greased rack in a shallow baking dish.
- In a large bowl, add the beef, egg, breadcrumbs, parsley flakes, allspice, nutmeg and pepper and mix till well combined.
- Make 1-inch balls from the mixture.
- Arrange the balls over the prepared rack in baking dish.
- Cook in the oven for about 15 minutes.
- Drain the pan liquid.
- In a large pan, mix together the remaining ingredients.
- Add the meatballs and bring to a boil.
- Reduce the heat and simmer, covered for about 30-35 minutes.
- Discard the bay leaf before serving.

Servings Per Recipe: 8

Timing Information:

Preparation	10 mins
Total Time	1 hr 5 mins

Nutritional Information:

Calories	309.4
Fat	15.0g
Cholesterol	85.4mg
Sodium	1647.8mg
Carbohydrates	22.2g
Protein	22.0g

* Percent Daily Values are based on a 2,000 calorie diet.

GERMAN CHEDDAR EGG NOODLES

Ingredients

- 8 oz. egg dumpling noodles
- 1 lb. ground beef
- 16 oz. tomato sauce
- 1 tsp salt
- 1/4 tsp garlic salt
- 1/8 tsp pepper
- 2 C. sour cream
- 1/2 C. green onion, sliced
- 1 C. shredded cheddar cheese

Directions

- Set your oven to 350 degrees F before doing anything else and grease a 2 quart casserole dish.
- In a large pan of the lightly salted boiling water, prepare the egg noodles according to the package's directions.
- Drain well and keep aside.
- Heat a skillet on medium heat and cook the ground beef till browned completely.
- Drain the grease from the skillet.
- Stir in the tomato sauce, garlic salt, salt and pepper.

- In a bowl, mix together the sour cream, onions and noodles.
- In the prepared casserole dish, arrange the noodle mixture and beef mixture in layers, ending with the beef mixture.
- Sprinkle cheese on top and cook in the oven for about 20-25 minutes.

Servings Per Recipe: 4

Timing Information:

Preparation	5 mins
Total Time	30 mins

Nutritional Information:

Calories	830.7
Fat	51.8g
Cholesterol	214.4mg
Sodium	1536.6mg
Carbohydrates	51.5g
Protein	40.3g

* Percent Daily Values are based on a 2,000 calorie diet.

Christmas Bavarian Eggnog

Ingredients

- 1 quart eggnog
- 2 1/4 tsp unflavored gelatin
- 1/2 tsp vanilla
- 1 C. heavy cream

Directions

- In a microwave safe bowl, add 1/4 C. of the water and sprinkle with the gelatin.
- Keep aside for about 5 minutes.
- Now, microwave for about 10 seconds.
- Remove from the microwave and stir till dissolved completely.
- In a bowl, add the heavy cream and beat till soft peaks form.
- In a large bowl, place the eggnog, gelatin mixture and vanilla extract and beat till well combined.
- Add 1/3 of the whipped cream and beat till well combined.
- Gently, fold in the remaining cream.
- Divide mixture into serving bowls and refrigerate for at least 6 hours or overnight.

Servings Per Recipe: 6

Timing Information:

Preparation	15 mins
Total Time	6 hrs 15 mins

Nutritional Information:

Calories	369.3
Fat	27.3g
Cholesterol	154.2mg
Sodium	108.2mg
Carbohydrates	24.0g
Protein	8.0g

* Percent Daily Values are based on a 2,000 calorie diet.

German Green Beans

Ingredients

- 18 oz. frozen green beans
- 1/4 lb. turkey bacon
- 1/3 C. onion
- 4 oz. beer, optional
- 2 tbsp sugar
- 1/4 tsp salt
- 1/8 tsp white pepper
- 1 C. spaetzle noodles

Directions

- In a pan, add the beans and a small amount of water on a medium heat and bring to a boil.
- Reduce the heat and simmer, covered till tender.
- Remove from the heat and drain well.
- Heat a skillet on medium heat and cook the bacon and onions for about 8-10 minutes.
- Stir in the beer, sugar, salt and pepper and bring to a boil.
- Remove from the heat and stir in the the noodles.
- Place the noodles mixture over the beans and serve.
- Serve hot.

Servings Per Recipe: 8

Timing Information:

Preparation	20 mins
Total Time	40 mins

Nutritional Information:

Calories	104.1
Fat	6.5g
Cholesterol	9.6mg
Sodium	192.2mg
Carbohydrates	8.5g
Protein	2.7g

* Percent Daily Values are based on a 2,000 calorie diet.

Bavarian Cranberry Frosting

Ingredients

BAVARIAN

- 3/4 C. cold water
- 3 tbsp unflavored gelatin
- 4 C. eggnog
- 1/4 C. sugar
- 1/4 tsp nutmeg
- 1 C. whipping cream, whipped

SAUCE

- 3/4 C. sugar
- 1/2 C. water
- 1 C. whole berry cranberry sauce
- 1/4 C. water
- 1/2 tsp unflavored gelatin
- 1 orange, rind of
- 1/3 C. walnuts, chopped fine

Directions

- For the Bavarian: in a bowl, add the cold water and sprinkle with the gelatin. Keep aside till softened.

- In a pan, add 1 C. of the eggnog, sugar, nutmeg and gelatin mixture on low heat and cook till the gelatin is dissolved, stirring occasionally.
- remove from the heat and stir in remaining 3 C. of the eggnog.
- Refrigerate till set partially.
- Fold in the whipped cream.
- Transfer the mixture into a mold and refrigerate for about 6-8 hours.
- For the sauce: in a pan, add the sugar and 1/2 C. of the water and bring to a boil.
- Add the cranberries and cook for about 5 minutes.
- Meanwhile, in a bowl, add 1/4 c. of the cold water and sprinkle with the gelatin. Keep aside till softened.
- Add gelatin mixture into the cranberry mixture and stir to dissolve.
- Remove from the heat and stir in the orange rind and walnuts.
- refrigerate to chill completely.
- Serve the Bavarian alongside the sauce.

Servings Per Recipe: 6

Timing Information:

Preparation	15 mins
Total Time	15 mins

Nutritional Information:

Calories	619.5
Fat	31.6g
Cholesterol	154.2mg
Sodium	128.4mg
Carbohydrates	76.2g
Protein	11.5g

* Percent Daily Values are based on a 2,000 calorie diet.

BAVARIAN BANANAS

Ingredients

- 3 scoops sugar-free vanilla ice cream
- 1/2 banana
- sugar-free chocolate syrup, 1 healthy squirt
- 1 tsp Splenda sugar substitute
- 3 tbsp sugar-free strawberry jam
- 4 oz. milk

Directions

- In a blender, add all the ingredients and pulse on high speed for about 1 minute.
- Serve immediately.

Servings Per Recipe: 1

Timing Information:

Preparation	5 mins
Total Time	5 mins

Nutritional Information:

Calories	134.6
Fat	4.6g
Cholesterol	17.0mg
Sodium	60.3mg
Carbohydrates	20.2g
Protein	4.6g

* Percent Daily Values are based on a 2,000 calorie diet.

AUTHENTIC APPLE STRUDEL

Ingredients

- 8 C. flour
- 2 eggs
- 2 tbsp oil
- 2 1/2 C. warm water
- 1 pinch salt

APPLE FILLING

- 8 -10 tart apples
- sugar and cinnamon, to your taste and
- lightly dot all with melted butter

Directions

- In a bowl, add the flour, eggs, oil, water and salt and mix till a dough is formed.
- Divide the dough into 3 portions.
- Make a ball from each dough portion and coat each one with the oil.
- Keep aside for about 45 minutes.
- Set your oven to 350 degrees F and grease a baking dish.
- Arrange an old clean tablecloth on the table.
- Place a ball over the cloth and roll out as thin as possible.

- Coat each rolled dough portion with the melted butter generously during the rolling.
- Trim off the heavy edges.
- Sprinkle the rolled dough with the apples, some sugar, cinnamon and nuts and then, drizzle with a little melted butter.
- With the tablecloth, fold about 5-inch over toward the center on each side forming a frame around the dough.
- From the long side, Lift one side of the tablecloth and roll as long as your pan is.
- Seal the edges to secure the filling.
- Gently put rolled strudel into the prepared baking dish and cook in the oven for about 45-55 minutes.

Servings Per Recipe: 1

Timing Information:

Preparation	1 hr 30 mins
Total Time	2 hrs 15 mins

Nutritional Information:

Calories	1593.5
Fat	16.3g
Cholesterol	124.0mg
Sodium	116.4mg
Carbohydrates	321.6g
Protein	39.8g

* Percent Daily Values are based on a 2,000 calorie diet.

Bavarian Potato Chowder

Ingredients

- 8 C. cubed potatoes, peeled and cooked tender crisp with 1/4 c water from cooking reserved
- 1 medium onion, chopped
- 3 C. sliced carrots, cooked tender crisp
- 4 celery ribs, chopped fine ly
- 1 lb. savoy cabbage, shredded and cooked until tender 1/4 c water from cooking reserved
- 1 (20 oz.) cans Worthington veja-links, chopped into rounds with 1/4 c of liquid reserved
- 2 1/2 tsp caraway seeds
- 1 (15 oz.) cans cream-style corn
- 1 C. half-and-half
- milk, enough to make soup
- sour cream (to garnish)
- green onion, slices (to garnish)
- pepper, to sprinkle over top of soup bowl

Directions

- In a pan, melt the margarine and and sauté the onion and celery till tender.

- In a crock pot, add the onion mixture and remaining all cooked vegetables.
- Add half and half, milk and the reserved liquids from the cooked vegetables and stir well.
- Set the crock pot on High and cook, covered for about 3 hours, stirring occasionally.
- Transfer the chowder into serving bowls and serve with a topping of the sour cream green onions.

Servings Per Recipe: 5

Timing Information:

Preparation	20 mins
Total Time	3 hrs 20 mins

Nutritional Information:

Calories	377.8
Fat	6.6g
Cholesterol	17.9mg
Sodium	374.2mg75.0g
Carbohydrates	10.8g
Protein	377.8

* Percent Daily Values are based on a 2,000 calorie diet.

How to Make Sauerkraut

Ingredients

- 16 oz. sauerkraut, rinsed and drained
- 1 C. dry white wine
- 1/2 C. onion, chopped
- 1/2 C. apple, peeled and chopped
- 10 juniper berries, cracked
- salt & freshly ground black pepper
- 1 tbsp olive oil

Directions

- In a large pan, add all the ingredients and simmer for about 30-45 minutes

Servings Per Recipe: 4

Timing Information:

Preparation	10 mins
Total Time	40 mins

Nutritional Information:

Calories	117.8
Fat	3.5g
Cholesterol	0.0mg
Sodium	792.2mg
Carbohydrates	10.8g
Protein	1.3g

* Percent Daily Values are based on a 2,000 calorie diet.

RASPBERRY BAVARIAN CREAME

Ingredients

- 2 C. milk
- 1 tsp vanilla extract
- 4 egg yolks
- 1/2 C. sugar
- 2 tbsp unflavored gelatin (powder form)
- 1/2 C. cold water
- 2 1/2 C. heavy cream
- 1 pint raspberries (fresh)
- 1/2 C. sugar
- 1/3 C. red Burgundy wine

Directions

- For the Bavarian cream: in a bowl, add the heavy cream and beat till soft peaks are formed.
- Refrigerate till using.
- In a bowl, dissolve the gelatin in 1/2 C. of the cold water and keep aside for about 10 minutes.
- Arrange a fine mesh strainer inside a medium bowl.
- Fill a larger bowl with the ice water.
- In a medium span, add the milk and bring to a boil.

- Remove from the heat and keep aside.
- In a bowl, add the eggs and sugar and with a wire whisk, beat till thickened and pale yellow in color.
- Add a 1/4 C. of the hot milk to the egg mixture, stirring continuously.
- Add the yolks mixture into the milk in the pan over very low heat and cook till the mixture becomes thick, stirring continuously.
- Through the mesh strainer, strain the mixture into the bowl.
- Remove the strainer.
- Add the softened gelatin and beat till the gelatin is dissolved.
- Add the vanilla extract and mix well.
- Place the bowl into the larger bowl of ice water and stir till the mixture just begins to thick and cool.
- Immediately, remove the bowl of the custard from th ice water.
- Fold in the whipped cream.
- Transfer the custard into a serving bowl and refrigerate to chill.
- Meanwhile for the raspberry sauce: in a blender, add the raspberries and pulse till pureed.
- Through a sieve, strain the raspberry puree.
- In a pan, add 1/2 C. of the sugar, 1/3 C. of the red wine and a small piece of the lemon rind and bring to a boil.
- Add the raspberry puree and cook for about 3-4 minutes.

- Refrigerate to chill before serving.
- Serve the custard with the topping of the raspberry sauce.

Servings Per Recipe: 2

Timing Information:

Preparation	20 mins
Total Time	1 hr 20 mins

Nutritional Information:

Calories	1806.8
Fat	128.1g
Cholesterol	819.3mg
Sodium	263.7mg
Carbohydrates	140.8g
Protein	26.8g

* Percent Daily Values are based on a 2,000 calorie diet.

BAVARIAN HOT CHUCK STEW

Ingredients

- 5 lb. chuck roast
- 2 tbsp canola oil
- 1 tbsp cinnamon
- 1 tbsp sugar
- 1 tbsp vinegar, Apple Cider
- 1 C. water
- 12 oz. beer
- 1 C. tomato sauce
- 2/3 C. yellow onion, chopped
- 1 bay leaf
- 1 1/2 tsp salt
- flour (to dust meat and to thicken gravy as needed)
- salt
- pepper

Directions

- Sprinkle the meat with the flour, salt and pepper evenly.
- In a Dutch oven, heat the oil and sear the meat till browned completely.

- In a bowl, add the remaining ingredients except the and mix well.
- Place the mixture over the meat and simmer , covered for about 3 hours.
- Stir in the flour. and cook till mixture becomes thick.

Servings Per Recipe: 8

Timing Information:

Preparation	20 mins
Total Time	3 hrs 20 mins

Nutritional Information:

Calories	468.5
Fat	20.7g
Cholesterol	187.1mg
Sodium	829.4mg
Carbohydrates	7.7g
Protein	60.7g

* Percent Daily Values are based on a 2,000 calorie diet.

BAVARIAN APPLESAUCE SAUERKRAUT FRITTERS

Ingredients

- 1 1/2 lb. ground beef
- 1/2 C. applesauce
- 1/3 C. dry breadcrumbs
- 1/3 C. finely chopped onion
- 1 large egg
- 1 tsp salt
- 1/2 tsp allspice
- 1 (16 oz.) can drained sauerkraut

Directions

- In a bowl, add all the ingredients except the sauerkraut and mix till well combined.
- Make 6 (3/4-inch thick) patties from the mixture.
- Heat a large nonstick skillet over medium heat and cook the patties till browned from both sides.
- Drain off the excess fat from the skillet.
- Place the sauerkraut over the patties and simmer, covered for about 15 minutes.

Servings Per Recipe: 6

Timing Information:

Preparation	10 mins
Total Time	30 mins

Nutritional Information:

Calories	820.7
Fat	81.6g
Cholesterol	143.3mg
Sodium	479.2mg
Carbohydrates	9.5g
Protein	11.3g

* Percent Daily Values are based on a 2,000 calorie diet.

Bavarian Egg Noodles

Ingredients

- 1 boneless beef chuck roast (about 3 lb.)
- 1/2 C. chopped onion
- 1 (8 oz.) cans tomato sauce
- 3/4 C. beef broth
- 1 1/4 C. water
- 3 tsp cooking oil
- 2 tsp sugar
- 1 tsp vinegar
- 2 tsp salt
- 1 tsp cinnamon
- 1/2 tsp ground ginger
- 1/2 tsp pepper
- 1 bay leaf
- cornstarch (and water to thicken juices if desired)
- hot wide egg noodles

Directions

- In a large pan, heat the oil and sea the meat till browned.
- In a bowl, mix together all the ingredients except cornstarch.

- Place the mixture over the meat and bring to a boil.
- Reduce the heat and simmer, covered for about 2 1/2-3 hours.
- Remove meat from the pan and discard the bay leaf.
- You can thicken the pan juices with the cornstarch and water.
- Serve the meat and gravy over the hot egg noodles.

Servings Per Recipe: 6

Timing Information:

Preparation	20 mins
Total Time	3 hrs 20 mins

Nutritional Information:

Calories	268.1
Fat	12.1g
Cholesterol	105.6mg
Sodium	1218.1mg
Carbohydrates	5.7g
Protein	34.8g

* Percent Daily Values are based on a 2,000 calorie diet.

Bavarian Dinner Rolls

Ingredients

- 5 1/2 C. bread flour (divided)
- 1/4 oz. dry yeast
- 1 tbsp sugar
- 1 1/2 tsp salt
- 1 1/2 C. warm water
- 1 tsp malt extract or 1 tsp molasses
- 1 egg
- 1 egg white
- 1 tbsp shortening
- cornmeal, for dusting

Directions

- In a bowl, mix together about 4 1/2 C. of the flour, yeast, sugar and salt.
- Add the warm water and malt extract and with a flat paddle beater, mix till a smooth.
- and heavy mixture is formed.
- Add the egg, egg white and shortening and beat till smooth.
- Now, attach to dough hook.

- Add the remaining flour, 1/4 C. at a time and mix till a non-sticky dough is formed.
- With a dough hook, knead for about 8-10 minutes.
- Place the dough into a greased bowl.
- With a plastic wrap, cover the bowl tightly and keep in a warm place for about 1 hour.
- Uncover the bowl and with your fingers tips, punch down the dough.
- With a plastic wrap, cover the bowl tightly and keep in a warm place for about 45 minutes.
- Place the dough onto a smooth surface and loosely roll into a 12-inch long cylinder.
- With a sharp knife cut the cylinder into 12 equal pieces
- Shape each pieces into a smooth ball.
- With a plastic wrap, cover the bowl loosely and keep aside for about 5 minutes.
- With your hand, flatten each ball into 1/2-inch thickness.
- Dust the rolls with the cornmeal lightly.
- With the handle of a wooden spoon, make a deep indentation in the top of each roll and press firmly and deeply, almost to the bottom.
- Arrange the rolls onto a parchment lined baking sheet, face down.
- With a lint free towel, cover the rolls loosely and keep aside in room temperature for about 40 minutes.
- Set your oven to 450 degrees F and arrange a rack the bottom of the oven.

- In a baking dish, add C. of hot water in place in the oven for about 5 minutes to form the steam.
- Uncover the rolls and carefully, turn them right side up.
- Drizzle the rolls with the hot water slightly.
- Place the baking sheet of the rolls on the middle shelf of the oven for about 3 minutes.
- Drizzle the oven walls with water lightly.
- Cook for about 20-25 minutes, turning the sheet around once in the middle way.
- Remove the rolls from the oven and keep onto a cooling rack to cool completely before serving.

Servings Per Recipe: 12

Timing Information:

Preparation	2 hrs 45 mins
Total Time	3 hrs 10 mins

Nutritional Information:

Calories	233.4
Fat	2.0g
Cholesterol	17.6mg
Sodium	303.3mg
Carbohydrates	45.5g
Protein	7.0g

* Percent Daily Values are based on a 2,000 calorie diet.

German Pancakes

Ingredients

- 4 eggs, beaten
- 2 C. milk
- 1 1/2 C. flour
- 2 tbsp vegetable oil
- 1/2 tsp salt
- 2 tbsp sugar

Directions

- In a pan, add all the ingredients and mix till just combined with some lumps.
- In a skillet, melt the butter.
- Place about 1/2 C. of the mixture in a circle and cook till bubbly and light brown from both sides.
- Top with your favorite topping and roll before serving.

Servings Per Recipe: 1

Timing Information:

Preparation	5 mins
Total Time	20 mins

Nutritional Information:

Calories	202.3
Fat	8.2g
Cholesterol	101.5mg
Sodium	211.2mg
Carbohydrates	24.0g
Protein	7.5g

* Percent Daily Values are based on a 2,000 calorie diet.

Handmade Bavarian Bread

Ingredients

- 5 1/2 C. unbleached alltrumps high gluten bread flour
- 2 1/2 C. dark rye flour
- 3 1/4 tsp salt
- 2 tbsp dry yeast
- 2 tsp sugar
- 22 oz. water

Directions

- In a large bowl, mix together the white flour and dark rye flour.
- In a second bowl, mix together the dry yeast and 2 tsp of the sugar.
- Add 1/2 C. of the lukewarm water and mix till the the sugar is dissolved.
- Make a small well in center of the flour mixture.
- Add the yeast mixture into the well and keep aide, covered for about 15 minutes.
- Add in 3 1/4 tsp of the salt and with your hands, knead well.
- Add the remaining lukewarm water and knead till a smooth and sleek dough is formed.

- Cover the bowl and keep and place in a warm place for about 30 minutes.
- Set your oven to 120 degrees F.
- with your hands, knead the dough one more time.
- Shape the dough into a loaf. With a damp cloth, cover the dough and place in the preheated oven for about 40 minutes.
- Remove the dough from the oven.
- Now, set the oven to 480 degrees F and lightly grease a baking sheet. Arrange the rack in the second from bottom portion.
- Place the loaf onto the prepared baking sheet and coat the loaf loaf with the water.
- Arrange the baking sheet in the oven.
- In a broiler pan, add 2 C. of the water and place in the bottom rack of the oven to create steam.
- Immediately close the door of the oven and cook for about 10 minutes.
- Now, set your oven to 375 degrees and cook for abut 30-35 minutes.
- Remove bread from the oven.
- Rub flour over the bread and keep onto wire rack to cool.

Servings Per Recipe: 12

Timing Information:

Preparation	2 hrs
Total Time	2 hrs 30 mins

Nutritional Information:

Calories	317.3
Fat	1.6g
Cholesterol	0.0mg
Sodium	634.7mg
Carbohydrates	65.1g
Protein	12.5g

* Percent Daily Values are based on a 2,000 calorie diet.

OLD GERMAN SEMI-SWEET BROWNIES

Ingredients

- 1 (18 oz.) packages German chocolate cake mix
- 1/3 C. milk
- 1/4 C. butter, softened
- 1 egg
- 1 C. semi-sweet chocolate chips
- 1/2 C. chopped walnuts

Directions

- Set your oven to 350 degrees F before doing anything else and grease a 13x9-inch baking dish.
- In a large bowl, add the cake mix, milk, butter and eggs and with an electric mixer, beat till well combined.
- Fold in he chocolate chips and walnuts.
- Place the mixture into he prepared pan evenly and with the back f the spoon, smooth the surface.
- Cook in the oven for about 20-30 minutes.
- Remove from the oven and keep onto the wire rack to cool completely.
- Cut into squares and serve.

Servings Per Recipe: 24

Timing Information:

Preparation	10 mins
Total Time	40 mins

Nutritional Information:

Calories	157.0
Fat	7.9g
Cholesterol	13.3mg
Sodium	195.4mg
Carbohydrates	22.0g
Protein	1.9g

* Percent Daily Values are based on a 2,000 calorie diet.

Bavarian Kiwis

Ingredients

- 1 lemon jelly
- 1 (8 oz.) cans chilled evaporated low-fat milk
- 1 (15 oz.) cans crushed pineapple in juice
- 2 kiwi fruits
- chocolate, grated

Directions

- In a bowl, dissolve the jelly in half of the required boiling water. Keep aside to cool.
- Add the can of pineapple with all the juice and mix.
- In another bowl, add the evaporated milk and beat well.
- Fold the milk into the jelly mixture till it changes the color.
- Refrigerate till set before serving.
- Serve with a garnishing of the kiwi and chocolate.

Servings Per Recipe: 6

Timing Information:

Preparation	15 mins
Total Time	2 hrs 15 mins

Nutritional Information:

Calories	56.5
Fat	0.1g
Cholesterol	0.0mg
Sodium	1.4mg
Carbohydrates	14.5g
Protein	0.5g

* Percent Daily Values are based on a 2,000 calorie diet.

German Bartlett Tarts

Ingredients

MIX

- 1/2 C. butter
- 1/3 C. sugar

ADD

- 1 tsp vanilla
- 3/4 C. flour
- 2/3 C. nuts

FILLING

- 1 (8 oz.) packages cream cheese
- 1 egg
- 1/4 C. sugar
- 1 tsp vanilla

TOPPING

- 1 (15 oz.) cans Bartlett pears, sliced
- 1 tsp cinnamon

Directions

- Set your oven to 350 degrees F before doing anything else.

- For the bottom crust: in a bowl, mix together the butter and sugar.
- Add the vanilla, flour and nuts and mix well.
- Place the crumb mixture in a spring form pan and press to smooth the surface.
- Cook in the oven for about 10 minutes.
- Remove from the oven and keep aside.
- For the filling: in a bowl, add all the ingredients and beat till smooth.
- Place the filling mixture over the crust evenly.
- For the topping: Drain the pears and cut each pear half into eights.
- arrange pear pieces over the filling mixture and cook in the oven for about 40 minutes.

Servings Per Recipe: 8

Timing Information:

Preparation	15 mins
Total Time	1 hr 5 mins

Nutritional Information:

Calories	409.6
Fat	27.9g
Cholesterol	84.9mg
Sodium	279.1mg
Carbohydrates	36.2g
Protein	6.0g

* Percent Daily Values are based on a 2,000 calorie diet.

BAVARIAN CHOCOLATE BISCUIT PIE

Ingredients

- 180 g malt biscuits
- 80 g butter
- 1/4 C. milk
- 100 g chopped marshmallows
- 200 g good quality chopped dark chocolate
- 1 tsp unflavored gelatin, powder
- 300 ml whipped thickened cream
- 200 ml extra for decoration thickened cream
- chocolate shavings, to decorate

Directions

- Grease the bottom of an 8-inch spring form pan.
- In a food processor, add the biscuits and pulse till a fine crumb is formed.
- Add the melted butter and pulse till well combined.
- Place the crumb mixture into the prepared pan and press to smooth the surface.
- Refrigerate for about 30 minutes to firm.
- Add the milk, marshmallows and chocolate in a heatproof bowl, set over a pan of the simmering water and cook till smooth, stirring continuously.

- Remove the bowl from pan.
- Add the gelatin and 1 tbsp of the cold water in a heatproof bowl, set over a pan of the   simmering water and stir till gelatin dissolves completely.
- Add the gelatin mixture into the chocolate mixture and stir to combine.
- Keep aside to cool for about 30 minutes.
- Gently fold the whipped cream into the chocolate mixture.
- Place the cream mixture over the biscuit base and refrigerate, covered for about 4 hours to set.
- Place the extra cream over the pie evenly and serve with a topping of the shaved chocolate.

Servings Per Recipe: 8

Timing Information:

Preparation	20 mins
Total Time	4 hrs 20 mins

Nutritional Information:

Calories	480.8
Fat	46.9g
Cholesterol	109.2mg
Sodium	102.6mg
Carbohydrates	20.9g
Protein	5.8g

* Percent Daily Values are based on a 2,000 calorie diet.

BAVARIAN CHIVE AND TARRAGON SALAD

Ingredients

- 3/4 lb. beef summer sausage, or bratwurst
- 1 small red onion, minced
- 2 tbsp snipped chives
- 4 tbsp olive oil
- 2 tbsp tarragon vinegar
- 1 large dill pickle, chopped
- 2 tbsp German mustard
- salt and pepper
- paprika (to garnish)

Directions

- In a large serving bowl, add all the ingredients and mix well.
- Refrigerate for several hours or overnight before serving.

Servings Per Recipe: 3

Timing Information:

Preparation	10 mins
Total Time	10 mins

Nutritional Information:

Calories	386.2
Fat	29.9g
Cholesterol	62.3mg
Sodium	2136.1mg
Carbohydrates	4.8g
Protein	22.1g

* Percent Daily Values are based on a 2,000 calorie diet.

German Heavy Cream Pie

Ingredients

- 1 quart strawberry
- 1/2 C. sugar
- 3 tbsp cold water
- 2 tsp unflavored gelatin
- 3 tbsp boiling water
- 1 tbsp fresh lemon juice
- 1 C. cold heavy cream

Directions

- In a large bowl, add the strawberries and with a fork, crush them.
- Stir in the sugar and keep aside for about 30 minutes.
- In a bowl, add the cold water and sprinkle with the gelatin. Keep aside for about 5 minutes.
- Add the boiling water and stir till the gelatin is dissolved.
- Stir in the strawberries and lemon juice.
- Refrigerate till the mixture becomes thick.
- In a bowl, add the cream and beat till firm peaks form.
- Gently fold the whipped cream into the strawberry mixture.

- Place the mixture into the pie crust and refrigerate for at least 4 hours before serving.

Servings Per Recipe: 8

Timing Information:

Preparation	45 mins
Total Time	45 mins

Nutritional Information:

Calories	177.7
Fat	11.2g
Cholesterol	40.7mg
Sodium	13.4mg
Carbohydrates	19.3g
Protein	1.6g

* Percent Daily Values are based on a 2,000 calorie diet.

Bavarian Passion Pudding

Ingredients

- 7 1/2 oz. orange gelatin
- 1 1/2 C. boiling water
- 2 C. passion fruit juice
- 1 C. heavy cream
- GARNISH
- toasted coconut (optional)

Directions

- In a large bowl, dissolve the orange gelatin in the boiling water.
- Add the passion fruit juice and stir to combine.
- Refrigerate to chill completely.
- Remove from the refrigerator and stir the mixture well.
- In a bowl, add the cream and beat till stiff.
- Fold the whipped cream into the gelatin mixture.
- Refrigerate to chill completely.
- Serve with a garnishing of the coconut.

Servings Per Recipe: 4

Timing Information:

| Preparation | 10 mins |
| Total Time | 10 mins |

Nutritional Information:

Calories	407.6
Fat	22.0g
Cholesterol	81.5mg
Sodium	271.9mg
Carbohydrates	49.7g
Protein	5.3g

* Percent Daily Values are based on a 2,000 calorie diet.

How to Make a Potato Salad Bavarian

Ingredients

- 1 medium onion, chopped
- 1 cucumber, sliced thinly
- 5 -6 radishes, sliced thin
- 3 tbsp all-purpose flour
- 2/3 C. cider vinegar
- 1 C. water
- 1 tsp salt
- 1/2 tsp ground pepper
- 6 -8 C. potatoes, sliced, cooked and peeled

Directions

- In a pan, melt the butter and sauté the onion till tender.
- Add the flour and stir to combine.
- Add the cider vinegar and water and cook till the mixture becomes thick, stirring continuously.
- In a large serving bowl, mix together the potato, radishes, cucumbers, salt and pepper.
- Place the hot onion mixture over potato mixture and gently, stir to combine.

- Serve immediately.

Servings Per Recipe: 6

Timing Information:

Preparation	30 mins
Total Time	50 mins

Nutritional Information:

Calories	150.6
Fat	0.2g
Cholesterol	0.0mg
Sodium	402.4mg
Carbohydrates	33.1g
Protein	3.9g

* Percent Daily Values are based on a 2,000 calorie diet.

GERMAN DUMPLINGS

Ingredients

- 8 hard French rolls
- 2 eggs, whisked
- 1 C. whole milk, scalded
- 1 tsp kosher salt
- 1 large handful fresh parsley, chopped

Directions

- Cut the bread into 1/4-inch thick slices.
- In a large bowl, add the bread slices, eggs, parsley and kosher salt and mix well.
- In a pan, add the milk and heat to till very hot but not boiling.
- Add the milk over the bread mixture evenly.
- With a towel, cover the bowl and keep aside for a few minutes.
- With your hands, mix the bread mixture till just combined.
- With wet hands, make 6 equal sized balls from the mixture and refrigerate to chill for about 15-30 minutes or overnight.

- In a pan of salted boiling water, cook the dumplings for about 15-20 minutes.

Servings Per Recipe: 1

Timing Information:

Preparation	15 mins
Total Time	35 mins

Nutritional Information:

Calories	189.2
Fat	5.1g
Cholesterol	74.5mg
Sodium	638.8mg
Carbohydrates	27.4g
Protein	7.7g

* Percent Daily Values are based on a 2,000 calorie diet.

BAVARIAN PINEAPPLE SHELLS

Ingredients

- 1/4 oz. unflavored gelatin
- 1/4 C. cold water
- 1 C. pineapple juice, unsweetened
- 1/4 C. sugar
- 3/4 C. mango puree
- 1 C. heavy cream, whipped
- 1 pie shell (regular cooked)

Directions

- In a bowl, dissolve the gelatin in cold water and keep aside till softened.
- In a medium pan, add the sugar and pineapple juice on medium heat and cook till the sugar is dissolved, stirring continuously.
- In a large bowl, add the gelatin mixture, pineapple juice mixture and mango puree and beat till well combined.
- Refrigerate the mixture till set partially.
- Fold the whipped cream into mango puree mixture.
- Place the mixture into the pie shell evenly and refrigerate to chill before serving.

Servings Per Recipe: 1

Timing Information:

Preparation	15 mins
Total Time	15 mins

Nutritional Information:

Calories	2154.6
Fat	148.5g
Cholesterol	326.0mg
Sodium	1047.7mg
Carbohydrates	189.4g
Protein	23.8g

* Percent Daily Values are based on a 2,000 calorie diet.

BAVARIAN CHOCOLATE CHEESE TRUFFLES

Ingredients

- 1 (18 1/4 oz.) boxes chocolate cake mix
- 2 (3 oz.) boxes raspberry Jell-O gelatin
- 12 oz. cream cheese, room temp
- 1 (12 oz.) frozen whipped topping, thawed and divided
- 1/4 C. frozen raspberries
- 1/4 C. granulated sugar

Directions

- Set your oven to 350 degrees F before doing anything else and grease and flour 11x15-inch jelly roll pans.
- Prepare the cake mix according to package's instructions.
- Divide the cake mixture into the prepared pans evenly and with the back of a spatula, smooth the surface.
- Cook in the oven for about 15 minutes or till a toothpick inserted in the center of cakes comes out clean.
- Remove from the oven and keep onto the wire rack to cool in the pan for about 5-10 minutes.
- Carefully, invert the cakes onto the wire rack to cool completely.

- In a bowl, dissolve the gelatin into 1 2/3 C. of the boiling water and keep aside for about 2 minutes.
- In a food processor, add the cream cheese and pulse for about 1 minute.
- Add the gelatin mixture and pulse for about 1 minute.
- Transfer the gelatin mixture into a large bowl.
- With a rubber spatula, gently fold in 4 C. of the whipped topping.
- Place the gelatin mixture over each cake evenly and refrigerate to chill for about 15 minute.
- Place 1 cake layer over second cake layer.
- Spread remaining whipped topping on top of the cake evenly.
- In a bowl, add the granulated sugar and roll the frozen raspberries in it.
- Cut the cake into equal sized squares and top with the raspberries.

Servings Per Recipe: 24

Timing Information:

Preparation	15 mins
Total Time	1 hr

Nutritional Information:

Calories	224.9
Fat	11.9g
Cholesterol	15.5mg
Sodium	256.4mg
Carbohydrates	28.5g
Protein	3.0g

* Percent Daily Values are based on a 2,000 calorie diet.

BAVARIAN VEGGIE SOUP

Ingredients

- 6 tbsp unsalted butter
- 4 carrots, cut into 3/8 inch thick rounds
- salt & freshly ground black pepper
- 1/4 C. finely chopped fresh parsley leaves
- 1 large celery root, peeled and sliced 1/4 inch thick
- 1 parsley root, peeled and sliced 1/4 inch thick
- 4 leeks, split lengthwise, washed well, and sliced
- 1 small cauliflower, broken into florets
- 1/2 lb. sugar snap pea, tough strings removed
- 1/2 lb. green beans, ends trimmed and cut into 1 inch pieces
- 1/2 head savoy cabbage, damaged outer leaves discarded, cored, and thinly sliced
- 1 lb. potato, peeled and sliced 1/4 inch thick
- 1 1/2 C. water

Directions

- In a large casserole, melt 3 tbsp of the butter on medium-high heat and remove from the heat.

- In the bottom of the casserole, arrange the carrots in a layer and sprinkle with the salt, pepper and a little of the parsley.
- Top with the layer of the celery root, followed by the layers of the parsley root, leeks, cauliflower florets, sugar snap pea, green beans, savoy cabbage and potato, sprinkling each layer with the salt, pepper and parsley.
- Place the remaining 3 tbsp of the butter over the potatoes in the form of the dots.
- Place the water over the vegetables.
- Cover the casserole tightly and bring to a boil.
- Reduce the heat to low and simmer for about 1 hour.

Servings Per Recipe: 8

Timing Information:

Preparation	20 mins
Total Time	1 hr 20 mins

Nutritional Information:

Calories	187.4
Fat	9.0g
Cholesterol	22.9mg
Sodium	48.3mg
Carbohydrates	25.2g
Protein	3.9g

* Percent Daily Values are based on a 2,000 calorie diet.

BAVARIAN CUTLETS

Ingredients

- 1 1/4 lb. boneless pork chops, 1/2 inch thick, or chicken cutlets
- 2 tbsp flour
- 1 tsp butter
- 1/2 C. green onion, chopped
- 2 garlic cloves, minced
- 8 oz. mushrooms, sliced
- 1/2 tsp thyme
- 8 oz. beer, room temperature, optional
- salt
- fresh ground black pepper
- 1 lb. buttered noodles, cooked (optional)
- fresh parsley, minced (optional)

Directions

- Coat the chops with the flour lightly.
- In a nonstick skillet, melt the butter on medium-high heat and sear the chops till browned from both sides.
- Transfer the chops onto a plate.
- In the same skillet, add the mushrooms, green onion, garlic and thyme and sauté for about 2-3 minutes.

- Stir in the cooked chops and beer and bring to a boil.
- Reduce the heat and simmer, covered for about 7-8 minutes.
- Stir in the salt and pepper and remove from the heat.
- Garnished with the parsley and serve alongside the buttered noodles.

Servings Per Recipe: 4

Timing Information:

Preparation	15 mins
Total Time	30 mins

Nutritional Information:

Calories	286.6
Fat	11.0g
Cholesterol	97.4mg
Sodium	83.9mg
Carbohydrates	8.3g
Protein	33.3g

* Percent Daily Values are based on a 2,000 calorie diet.

Bavarian Coconut Truffles

Ingredients

- 1 1/2 tbsp gelatin
- 4 tbsp coconut milk
- 1 (14 oz.) cans sweetened condensed milk
- 1 C. coconut milk
- 1/2 C. sugar
- 4 egg yolks
- 1 crème fraîche, Alouette Cuisine
- 7 oz. shredded coconut (toasted)

Directions

- In a bowl, dissolve the gelatin into 4 tbsp of the coconut milk. Keep aside to bloom.
- In a pan, add the condensed milk and remaining coconut milk on medium-high heat and bring to a gentle boil.
- In a bowl, add the sugar and egg yolks and beat well.
- Add a small amount the hot milk mixture into the egg yolk mixture and beat well.
- Slowly, add the egg yolk mixture into the milk mixture and cook for about 5-7 minutes, stirring continuously.
- Remove from the heat and stir in the gelatin mixture.

- Transfer the mixture into a bowl and refrigerate till the mixture begins to gel.
- In another bowl, add the crème fraîche and beat till soft peaks form.
- In the bowl of gel mixture, fold in crème fraiche.
- Immediately, place the mixture into your favorite molds and refrigerate overnight.
- Remove from the molds and serve with a topping of the shredded coconut.

Servings Per Recipe: 8

Timing Information:

Preparation	15 mins
Total Time	8 hrs 15 mins

Nutritional Information:

Calories	432.3
Fat	22.8g
Cholesterol	99.8mg
Sodium	139.5mg
Carbohydrates	52.6g
Protein	7.7g

* Percent Daily Values are based on a 2,000 calorie diet.

BAVARIAN SWEDISH MEATBALL

Ingredients

- 1 (6 -8 oz.) bags frozen precooked meatballs, thawed
- 1 medium onion, sliced
- 1/4 C. brown sugar, packed
- 3 tbsp beef and onion soup mix
- 1 (12 oz.) bottles beer, optional

Directions

- In a slow cooker, add all the ingredients and gently, stir to combine.
- Set the crock pot on Low and cook, covered for about 5-6 hours.
- Serve immediately.

Servings Per Recipe: 10

Timing Information:

Preparation	5 mins
Total Time	6 hrs 5 mins

Nutritional Information:

Calories	40.6
Fat	0.0g
Cholesterol	0.0mg
Sodium	3.4mg
Carbohydrates	7.6g
Protein	0.2g

* Percent Daily Values are based on a 2,000 calorie diet.

Beef Rolls of Bacon, Onions, and Pickles

(Rouladen Bavarian)

Ingredients

- 1 1/2 lbs flank steak, 1/4 inch fillets, 3 inches in width
- German stone ground mustard, to taste
- 1/2 lb thick sliced turkey bacon
- 2 large onions, sliced
- 1 (16 oz.) jar dill pickle slices
- 2 tbsps butter
- 2 1/2 C. water
- 1 cube beef bouillon

Directions

- Top each piece of steak with mustard then layer: onions, pickles, and bacon on each.
- Shape the filet into a roll then place a toothpick in each to preserve the structure.
- Brown your steaks in butter then add in 2.5 C. of water and bouillon.

- Mix the bouillon and water together and then gently boil the rolls for 60 mins with a low level of heat.
- Enjoy.

Amount per serving (6 total)

Timing Information:

Preparation	20 m
Cooking	1 h 10 m
Total Time	1 h 30 m

Nutritional Information:

Calories	264 kcal
Fat	17.4 g
Carbohydrates	7.7g
Protein	19.1 g
Cholesterol	59 mg
Sodium	1450 mg

* Percent Daily Values are based on a 2,000 calorie diet.

BAVARIAN EMPANADAS

Ingredients

- 1/2 C. chopped onion
- 1 1/2 lbs lean ground beef
- 1 (16 oz.) can sauerkraut, drained and pressed dry
- 2 (8 oz.) cans refrigerated crescent rolls
- 1 (8 oz.) package shredded Cheddar cheese

Directions

- Set your oven to 350 degrees before doing anything else.
- Stir fry your beef and onions until the beef is fully done then remove all the excess oils before adding in your sauerkraut.
- Get everything hot and then shut the heat.
- Flatten your rolls and then place them into a casserole dish.
- Top the rolls with the onion mix and then layer the 2nd piece of dough on top.
- Crimp the edges of the two layers of dough together then top everything with some cheese.
- Cook the dish in the oven for 27 mins.
- Enjoy.

Amount per serving (6 total)

Timing Information:

Preparation	20 m
Cooking	25 m
Total Time	45 m

Nutritional Information:

Calories	674 kcal
Fat	42.3 g
Carbohydrates	32.5g
Protein	37.1 g
Cholesterol	114 mg
Sodium	894 mg

* Percent Daily Values are based on a 2,000 calorie diet.

THANKS FOR READING! JOIN THE CLUB AND KEEP ON COOKING WITH 6 MORE COOKBOOKS....

http://bit.ly/1TdrStv

To grab the box sets simply follow the link mentioned above, or tap one of book covers.

This will take you to a page where you can simply enter your email address and a PDF version of the box sets will be emailed to you.

Hope you are ready for some serious cooking!

http://bit.ly/1TdrStv

COME ON...
LET'S BE FRIENDS :)

We adore our readers and love connecting with them socially.

Like BookSumo on Facebook and let's get social!

Facebook

And also check out the BookSumo Cooking Blog.

Food Lover Blog